To Nicholas &
Andrew

♡
mommy
3/1990

ORVILLE'S OUTING

BONNIE TIMMONS

JONATHAN CAPE
THIRTY BEDFORD SQUARE LONDON

First published 1983
Copyright © by Bonnie Timmons 1983
Jonathan Cape Ltd, 30 Bedford Square, London WC1

British Library Cataloguing in Publication Data

Timmons, Bonnie
Orville's outing.
1. Title
813,.54 [J]   P Z 7
ISBN 0-224-02147-8

Printed in Great Britain by
W.S. Cowell Ltd, Buttermarket, Ipswich
for Sadie Fields Productions Ltd
866 United Nations Plaza, Suite 4030,
New York 10017 USA

Orville was very happy.

The sun rose daily.

The moon rose nightly.

One day Orville left his house
to see the world.

He walked past towns

and trees

and hills.

He passed by cows

and birds and flowers.

He walked on and on

until he met a little
yellow-haired girl.

He stopped.

He smiled his friendliest smile.
He said his friendliest "hello."

But the little girl ran away.

Orville walked on.

Then he saw a crowd of people.

"Hello," he said. "I'm Orville."

But to his surprise they laughed at him.

Orville ran away.

He ran and ran. Then he stopped. "I have an idea," said Orville. "I'll try to look like them."

But the more he tried to look
like them, the more they laughed.

He tried hiding behind trees

and paper bags,

and wearing masks.

But the people kept on laughing.

Orville went home.

He thought he would burst, he was
so sad and lonely.

He went into his house and looked out of the window.
But when he opened his beak to cry,
the most beautiful music came pouring
out. Even the birds stopped to listen.

So did the little yellow-haired girl
who was picking flowers in the forest.

She followed the sound of the music

until she came to Orville's window.
"Don't stop," she said. "It's beautiful."

Other people heard it. And soon a crowd had gathered to hear Orville's song.

And Orville just kept on singing.